About the Author

Michelle Hulford was born in Bolivia, South America to missionary parents and one of five brothers and sisters . From a very young age she wanted to teach children and was very creative .

Michelle studied Early Childhood Education in college, travelled to South Africa, Kenya and Tanzania in her gap year to work with orphaned children and taught at a pre-school in her hometown before studying creative writing and dance choreography at Bath Spa University.

Tragically, Michelle was killed in a car accident early summer of 2012, aged 21 . She was loved, admired and will be missed by many. Michelle was always full of life and her smile lit up the room and lifted everyone's heart. Michelle loved God, people, and especially children . Her heart's vision was to teach and serve the disadvantaged children of Africa and write children's novels .

Michelle was and still is an inspiration to all who knew her.

Dougie the Dino

Michelle Hulford

Zest Publishing

www.zestpublishing.com
www.michellehulford.com

First published by Zest Publishing in 2013

Printed and bound in Great Britain. Distributed worldwide
by the Ingram Content Group.

ISBN 978-0-9574502-3-3

I dedicate this story to my wonderful and energetic
nephews, Oliver and Darwin whom I think the world of
and love .
Your fascination for dinosaurs inspired me to write you a
little story. I hope you like it and maybe, one day you can
tell more about Dougie the dinosaur as he grows up .

All my love and hugs

Auntie Michelle

This story is about a baby dinosaur called Dougie.

Dougie was different to the other dinosaurs in his family.

He didn't know why he was different, so one day he decided to go and find out.

Dougie started off trying to be like his Daddy and Mummy.
They were having lunch.
Daddy Dino was pulling big, green leaves off a tall tree,
while Mummy Dino munched on sweet yellow leaves.

Dougie felt hungry, so he tried to reach the top of the
tree but this only made his neck hurt.
He even went on tiptoes, but instead of getting higher he
tripped and ended up in a messy heap on the ground

Poof!

Since Dougie didn't have a long neck like them he
decided to visit Auntie Triceratop.

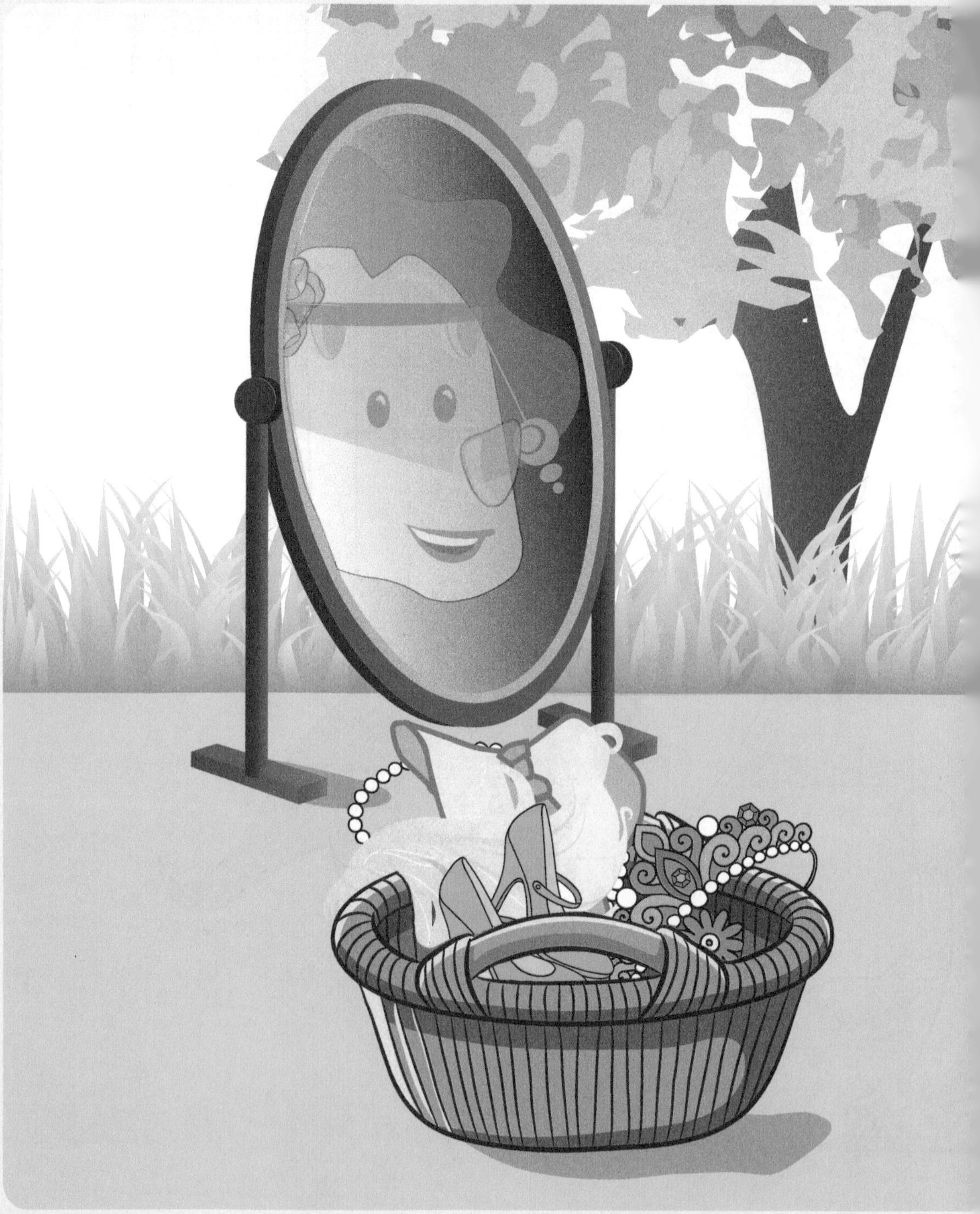

...tie Triceratop was looking in the mirror when Dougie arrived.

...llo Dougie!" she called. "Hi Auntie Triceratop. What are you doing today?" he asked.

...getting ready for a party," she said as she stuck a flower to one of her horns. She
...put a pink head band on and smiled.

...my friend's birthday, would you like to come?"

...gie felt so excited he couldn't stop his feet from jumping up and down.

...s please!"

...tie Triceratop brought out her dressing-up box and plonked it in front of him. Being
...to choose, Dougie got stuck. He didn't know what to pick. First Dougie took a blue
...ther hat. It looked good to begin with, but then it slipped and covered his eyes.
...good!

Next, he tried a curly wig.
He walked back and forth with the curls
dragging behind him until one got caught!

WOOSH!

The wig was yanked off and Dougie was
left hairless.

"These won't do!" laughed Auntie
Triceratop, "And I'm afraid I don't have
time to help. I must go now or I will be
late for the party!"

"Your cousin, Sauro is coming too, so why don't you go and find him. Then you can come together!"

Dougie shrugged and waved goodbye as his Auntie left, wearing even more jewels and feathers than he could count.

Dougie had some trouble finding Sauro. He wasn't in his resting place and he wasn't by the river. He wasn't at the eating ground and he wasn't with anyone else. Instead, Dougie found him hiding under a bush!

"What are you doing under here?" asked Dougie.
"Shhh," whispered Sauro, "I'm on a secret mission!"

"What is the secret?"
"Well, I have to get to the party without anyone seeing me," explained Sauro.
Dougie wriggled into the bush to join in but, instead of being quiet, the bush rustled and a few branches snapped!

Some of the party guests looked around to see what was making the noise.

Sauro frowned and told Dougie that they had to run!

"Run as fast as you can Dougie!"

Sauro dashed off before Dougie could even ask where to run to!

So Dougie took a deep breath and started to run.

Dougie tried to keep up, but only got more and more tired. He just wasn't fast enough.

Poor Dougie wasn't doing so well trying to be like everyone else.

He stopped running and sat down. Rubbing his claws through the dirt he wished of a way to be big like Mummy and Daddy Dino. He then wished for a way to be stylish like Auntie Triceratop.

And when the thought of being fast came into his head, he just sighed and closed his eyes.

Just then, a large bird flew down in front of him and squawked very loudly. Dougie squinted and saw that it was Tutoe the messenger bird.

"I have a message for you, Dougie," he said in his most important voice. Dougie was very surprised to be getting a message!
"What is it?"
"If you follow that dust cloud your cousin left behind, you will find something you weren't expecting."

eally?" gasped Dougie, "What is it?"
...toe laughed, "That I can't tell you my friend, but
...rry along - it won't wait forever!"

...ougie jumped up and smiled - maybe his wishing
...ally had done something .

...toe squawked again and flew off towards the
...st cloud . Dougie followed behind and this time
...e didn't walk or run - this time, he skipped .

He skipped and he skipped as only a little dinosaur could.

And finally he made it!

The dust cloud disappeared and there in the clearing was everyone he knew!
A huge banner was tied between two tall trees and on it was painted,
"HAPPY BIRTHDAY DOUGIE "

"Surprise!" chirped Tutoe as he wizzed through the air. Dougie was so surprised -
he'd completely forgotten it was <u>his</u> birthday. Mummy and Daddy Dino were both
there with big smiles and Auntie Triceratop was there looking as fabulous as ever.
There were many others too and Cousin Sauro was running around making sure
everyone had drinks and food to eat.

"We love you, Dougie," said Daddy Dino as he gave Dougie a big hug .
"But," stammered Dougie, "I thought this party was for Auntie Triceratop's friend?"
"It is." She interrupted, "<u>You</u> are my friend!"

Surprise!

Dougie felt confused,
but when he saw
Mummy Dino bringing
him a huge leaf cake all
his worries flew away.
All the dinosaurs at the
party sang him 'Happy
Birthday' and enjoyed
eating lots and lots of
leaf cake.

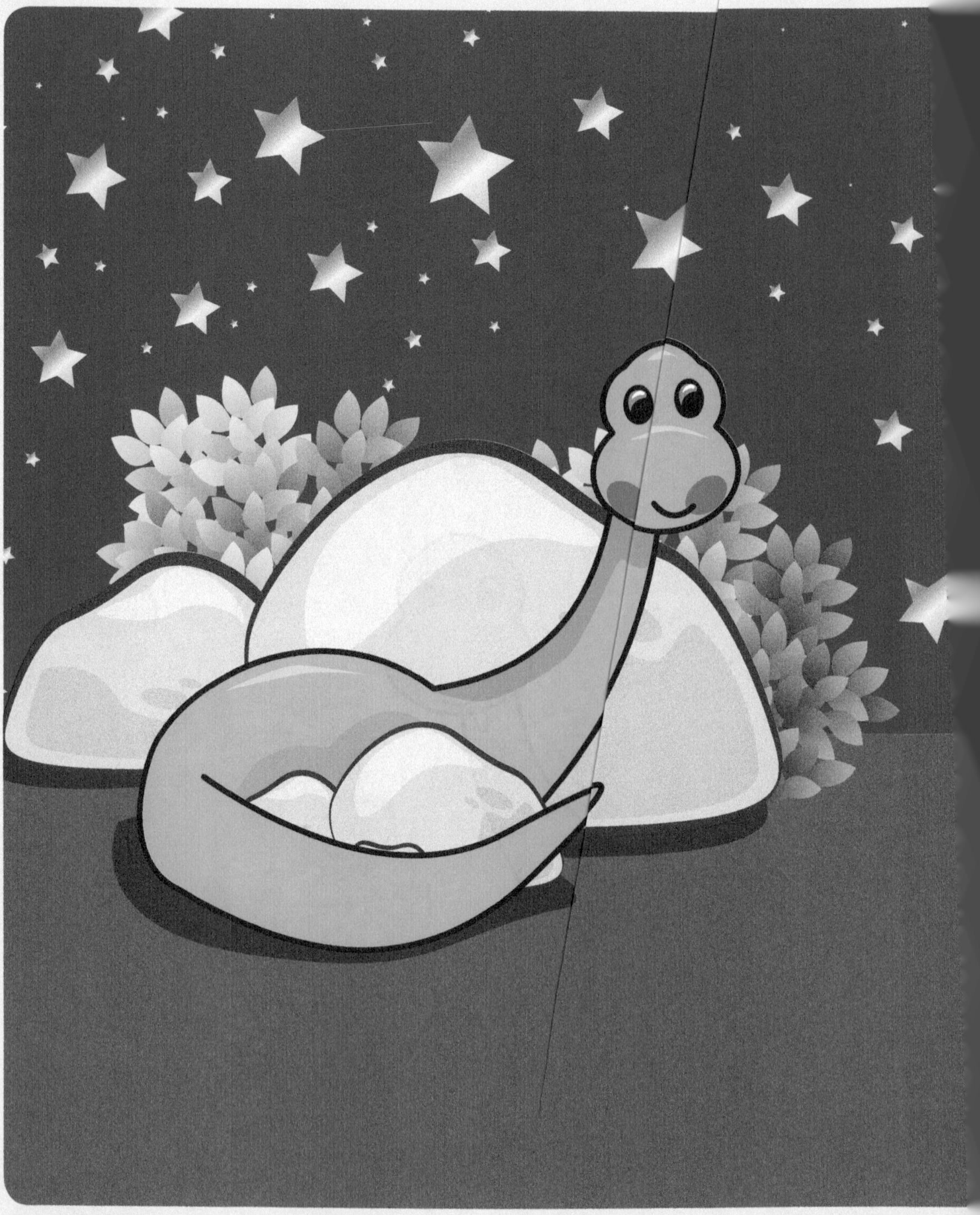

After eating and dancing it was time for bed . Before falling into a deep sleep, Dougie asked Mummy Dino, "Am I like all the other dinosaurs?"

Mummy Dino tucked Dougie into bed and smiled, "You don't have to be like the other dinosaurs, Dougie. You just have to be you. And that's what we love best."

Dougie smiled and knew that she was right.

"Good night," he whispered

"Good night, Dougie."

e sun went down and
stars came out.
ey twinkled like the candles on
of his cake Dougie curled into a ball
d yawned a big birthday yawn.
ke being Dougie," he thought to himself
d off he drifted into a peaceful sleep.

The above photo shows Michelle holding a child when she spent half her gap year in Kenya and Tanzania, helping and serving in orphanages and with children of the Maasai tribes. Since Michelle's premature departure, money has been raised to support three charities providing homes and education programmes in Ghana, Tanzania and Bolivia.
For further information you can go to:

www.michellehulford.com

Jackie Hulford
Editor
facebook.com/dougiethedino
spiritsoaring@hotmail.co.uk

Natalie Limbrey
Design and digital illustration
www.behance.net/natalielimbrey
natalielimbrey@live.co.uk